VITA

Poems by
Jorge Aguayo

CONTENTS

Introduction

Throughout life many events take place that one would like to change or just re-do. They form and mold character and personalities in positive and negative ways. Sometimes the things one witnesses and hears are so engraved in the memory that it feels like they occurred yesterday. To express what one feels is the hardest thing to do, but once that barrier is broken, what comes out of your gates is liberating.

The poems in this book are a compilation of words, thoughts, feelings, emotions and ideas that had been waiting to be expressed. They were suppressed for a long time until something happened that forced me to write them down. That was the most natural thing to do, since there was nobody around to share my feelings with. Many people have said that everyone has creative qualities, that we have an innate ability to do things. The issue is finding that ability and following through without fear. Others have said that when you bear it all, many will understand and empathize with you. They will have a connection, something relative that makes them feel like they are not the only ones.

A broad range of scenarios or situations have been used to picture what I call "VITA," or life. They vary from joy to anger, love and hate, peace and chaos and whatever can possibly fit in between. If one can imagine all the incidents, good and bad, that have occurred, a pretty hefty novel can be written. It takes a lot of reflecting and courage to put oneself in a position where one might feel vulnerable.

The poems in this book are definitely raw and naked. The best way, I believe, to share something very personal is by staying true to oneself and being completely honest. There is no other way artists, musicians, writers and poets can be.

My military background has given me a wealth of experience in many topics. And, participating in a war has provided me with a mindset that enabled me to start the process of writing my thoughts down. As a Marine I learned how to be an excellent infantryman, which takes a certain type of individual. The requirements are mental toughness and a hefty heart with a bit of motivation. At the same time, the world outside of the Marines is certainly difficult. This is where the real challenge is, adapting to a system that has been purged out of you. Communication skills, tact, patience and civility are very different between the Marines and the rest of the world.

Many times the question has been asked, "Why do we do what we do?" A philosopher might say that we do things for pleasure or pain. A psychologist will say that we do everything according to family and society. I'd say that we do things to survive. A man constructs a monument to let everyone know he is there and to assure that no one takes what he thinks belongs to him. A man will defend what he believes in, even if it means death; he will protect his beliefs so that others will not take them from him. He will sacrifice to feed himself and his own. The fear of not knowing what will happen next greatly affects the actions of a man. My reactions to all of these emotions are expressed in these poems.

Regimented Grunt

Perfection is what a grunt strives for. In garrison, your weapon has to be immaculate, every part of it has to function without any rust, carbon or debris. Your uniform must be better than perfect; it should be inspection ready at all times. The decks and the latrines should be shining as well; there is no excuse for having a dirty toilet. So what happens when you train for two straight weeks in the boonies? It doesn't matter; perfection is still required even if you haven't had a real shower for weeks. What do you do with all that perfection that seems to be coming out of every pore in your body? Why is this an important quality to have? How does this make you a better individual? How do you benefit from being "squared away"?

A young man is taught to do these things so that when he is faced with the biggest fight of his life, he can overcome. He is taught to fire a perfectly aimed shot, because it might be the last one he fires. Paying attention to small details can save many lives and everything has to be perfect, especially if you want to come back from patrol without a scratch. These qualities never go away. They are so embedded within your core that it becomes difficult not to react in that way. The frustration and struggle to separate myself from what I learned to be is described in the following verses. For many years the feeling of inadequacy lingered. I never learned how to cope with it.

Young Man

Young man
I have a question
Where are you going?

Fights are settled one way
You've chosen to walk that way
Mighty brave of you
To be in harms way

How did you get it?
To strap it on
Become an expert
And slay the evil one

Where did you find it?
Young man
To be so bold
Where did you find it?
To be so strong
Tell me
Where did you find it?
To stand so long

To you we raise our cup
For you we raise our voice
Because of you
More and more
Will make that choice

People come
People go
What you have
Is something much more

You've paid the price....

Fine example
Of the ultimate sacrifice

Young man
I have a question
Young man
Tell me
Where did you find it?

Under the Ground

A stream of light
In the distance
Becomes greater
As I crawl to get near

So bright
My eyes stare
A blinding silence
Pulsating in my face

Tell me why
Am I the only one?
That has to beg and plead
The only one to bleed
Why am I the only one?
To go under the ground

No silver or gold
No one to speak of
Not even a disease
To be sick of

I don't mind
It's just ridiculous
To get somewhere
And live forever

Sick and tired
Of being pushed
Exhausted
Of being taken under

Unknown and mistreated
Blind and hated
Dragging myself
Is how you want me

NO MAN'S LAND

Space between two fences
Where it's always lit up
Outside, it's a jungle
Inside, too many faces

When you think its safe inside
The darkness takes you
And the chaos on the inside
Surely will embrace you

In no man's land
You're guarded
In the light, you're sheltered
In no man's land
You're defended

The orders are to shoot
If you break the buffer zone
And if you cross the line
There is no way out

Where do you find yourself?
In the confusion
In the black
Or in the middle
With no life

ON TIME

Remember your crazy days
Pedaling your madness
Running and gunning your evil ways

Swift and silent
Like a crooked arrow
Holidays and trips you were always sent

Jumping off the ledge
Scraping your knee
Now you get out of bed leaning on a tree

Right on time
You've come up
Just in the nick of time
Better late then never
You're right on time

Provide more than you can
But you're between closing walls
And now you want to fight

Take what you don't need
Make space
Arrange it all in order
Nice and neat.

WAR FACE

There will come a time
When everything goes dark
All you will have
Is your sense of touch

They will come for you
Ask what side you belong to
Claim to protect you
And everything you're willing to fight for

Our opportunity
Your chance to start
To blow it all up

Show them your war face
Tell them of your uprising
Show them the blood
The start of a magnificent revolution

The want-to-be militants will run
Look for shelter within your gates
Turn them around
Let them use their forked tongue

There will come a time
When all are against you
All you will have
Is your right to fight

There will come a time
When they'll push back
And everything, everything
Will be pitch black.

Back In Again

It's my time to hold it down
The shame and ironies of my life
Don't laugh and can't feel it anymore
This one mind living in obscurity
Drench my despair because I'm not in it

To take comfort in this emptiness
And not seek the stillness
Want to quit
Just go through the motions
The life of every breath
The tear in every drop

Have all climbed inside again
Pull it back
I have no past and can't see the future
But I have many years in
I want to go back in again
Because.... I'm dying
Want to leave but you can't

Be yourself in your own shoes
But you're over it
You hate being home
Don't spend much time there
Rather be left alone
Your obligations have turned your hair gray
Selfish issues have made you blind

You want to wake up bright and early
Because you care.

I'll Go

What do you know
Of what I have done
What do you care
Of what's been going on

In my head
Over and Over again
That one night
I relive it
Over and Over again

Darker than black
A consuming fear
The call came in
For a brave volunteer

But can't take it anymore
I'll do it
I'll go
Gripping my sixteen
I'll dig through
So you won't have to

Big rats
Roaches in my cup
Found my peace
Giving it up

Took all night
Walking them in
Took the night
With my biggest fight

NORTH PARK

Sat alone on a miserable bench
Couldn't help noticing the stench
Of the dissection
Of the innocent mutilation

Tasted like dirty air
Couldn't keep from inhaling
Down deep
Where everything, everything stings

I didn't know
Couldn't understand
Why everything has an end

On a bus
Heading towards North Park
I discovered the fight
Never knew you can punch back

Smaller than a mouse
Never was found
Took it
And never, ever touched me

Slow and unshapely
Forever your life
Will be searching
For a chance to satisfy....
Satisfy

The mutilation.

An Ounce Of Motivation

Sometimes things don't work out the way you would like them to and you wonder why. So you search for reasons to look on the brighter side - some type of motivation to keep you moving. Sometimes it's a simple hello or maybe it's a promise you have to keep. I've always found it interesting how things occur at precisely the right moment. Someone always says something that catches your attention, changes your perspective. Or maybe they do something that affects your thinking and helps you to go in the right direction. It's always been a habit for me to pay attention to detail, to see and feel what is going on around me.

In all the chaos and confusion, I choose to find the beautiful things in this world. I look beyond the momentary setbacks and the injustice that exists in every corner. It takes is just an ounce to get me going. If the sun rises every morning, I will rise also. If it rains, I know it won't last forever. It feels so good to be free, to be able to maintain a positive state of mind where nothing or anyone can change it. You have to find it: passion, peace of mind, purpose, and the motivation to do something.

Beautiful Wings

Lift off
Carry us
With immediate support
Transport
Take it
To where I'll promote

Move.... Up
While we have a chance to
improve
Ascend
So far
As to receive no aid
Take off
Steal
No way to repeal
Aerial devices
Lofty
Grand and stately

Your turn
Take it up
Spread your beautiful wings
And inherit....
The wind

Turn me
Inside out
Into the superior
A realm
I may roam
That is much greater

Keep.... me
Less and less
To be more of who you are
Transfigure
The ordinary
Into something higher
Experience
Prevailing thoughts
To the next existence
Freely....
No compromise
Wait for me to rise

High and mighty
Soaring skyward
Elevated and towering
Affair.... in the air

RIDE

Out in the horizon

I see the beauty

Everything pure

In all its glory

Nothing to take
Capture a dream
Sit beside me
And take it all in
Come with me
Don't waste time
The sun will set
Soon we will be fine
Lets make a plan
I want to be there
Very necessary
To stay together
Lean way back
Let it come to you
The celestial sphere
As it passes through

Take pleasure
Satisfy your sense
Feel the power
It is yours to possess
Never look back
Have a good time
Its how you've traveled
You should keep in mind
We will take a ride
Down....
Down the road
To where it ends
No.... no one knows
Lets take a ride
Leave it all behind
Everything you have
Because
This is our time.

Thinking Silence

Around Midnight
Warm and cozy
I'm surrounded with the stillness
Of a restless mind

Echoes
Of an empty room
Resonate through the walls
For my heart to consume

They come back to me
Words and voices
Plans and choices
Have no meaning to me

Inches of separation
Between the two
Produced a love
Of a distant adventure

The absence of sound
Created a unity
A beautiful harmony
My heart and soul will move me

I'm thinking silence I slowly gravitate
Where nothing matters
Just a momentary.... Solitude.

Poem

Something made
Not with your hands
With your imagination
It was created eloquently
Expressed to move the world
To change my heart so intensely
The rhythm
Keeping everything together
This great beauty
To be likened forever
Like a poem without a verse
My voice cries out
To hear your song
Like a letter without words
My mind searches
Hoping you come along
Understand these things
Clearly made
To see not with your eyes
But with your heart's palpitation
The perfect work
Within you
Apparent to the most
Quietest sound within you.

FREE

Stood atop the mountain
Looking for an answer
Power moving through my soul
Inviting me to jump

Free in flight
To be free
To be free
Free to fly

How can I come down?
Where will I go?
Will I be able to see?
Or touch the heavens?

Free in flight
To be free
To be free
Free to fly

Something so strange
With the power to not feel
Rushing through my soul
Compelling me to stay

Free in flight
To be free
To be free
Free to fly

I can't tell you
How birds can fly
Don't really know
Why angels die.

More Than I Can Touch

There are so many things that I would love to control. I wish I had the power to change the weather, turn a wrong into a right, bring someone back to life, remove all the evil and keep people from fighting. What kind of life would that be, where everything is perfect and there is absolutely nothing to worry about? I don't live in paradise and I certainly can't make everything perfect. We try our hardest to make it seem that way. We make our homes our sanctuaries; we take our vacations to places where the smells and sights are breathtaking; and sometimes we surround ourselves with dreamy people. I've tried to make my environment perfect many times.

There is something much more powerful than you and I can ever comprehend. You can't touch it, you can't capture it in a bottle, you can't see it, you can't record it, and you definitely can't describe it. Energy exists between humans, nature and the galaxy that has been addressed by scientists and physicists. But how and why did it start? I've tried to understand, but my little brain can only compute so much. I've also tried to rationalize why things happen, but I just can't put my finger on it. You can ask why and how of pretty much everything, but an explanation might not be what we are looking for. It's, " I.... I will make sure this doesn't happen again!" We try to control everything.

ROSARY

I am more than what you think I am
Taught you everything I know
Don't you know
Took you under my shadow
Granted the ability
To express what you're willing to show

Look deep inside
Pull the malady from its root
Wipe your tears
Use them
Save yourself from your selfish thoughts
Plant your tree somewhere else

Kiss my hand
Raise it to your crown
Take my fist
Place it on your face
Embrace me
Tell me how much you love it

Dumb and unfounded
I must leave you
One of great wrath
Bitterness and laziness
I will not rescue you
Because I will have to do it over and over again

What we want....

 Is what we never had Where do you start
When you don't know how
 Begin to understand
Why we cried as babes
Approach with gracious tolerance
As you walk in shallow graves

Unwritten Common

Between you and I
Unspoken actions
That led us to pleasure and pain

Momentary Phases
Can't be separated
Cannot be permanently attached

Against us all
Something verbally understood
Customary and accepted

Related to the world
Near perfection with you
Attracted by the energy
That consumes all around you

Invisible to my eyes
Affections to my soul
Penetrating through the layers

Vapors flowing from the blood
That run along the creases
Around the bend
Of your existence.

Eddie's Song

On his knees against a dumpster
Something wicked pierced his right temple
Gravel under his fingernails showed signs of a struggle
No more in this world will you battle

A clean and pure teardrop
And the world flushed it away
It takes the beauty of a child
Hardens it up and casts it away

Just like Eddie's song
The kid finally spoke in class
As he walked through the garden of stone
With indifference on his back

Look in his eyes
Tell him you love him
It's what he deserves
And don't leave him.... Don't leave him
All alone

Innocence and righteousness
Never had a chance
Your talent and fortune
We knew.... Would never last

Nothing more to say
Listen to his song
Be watchful of the signs
And don't take too long.

Mediocre

Always wanted to stand
Never needed your help
To keep my composure
And never take your hand
Balancing on a wire
As far as I could walk
Trying to keep my poise
And my head on a level
Under my skin
I live in great turmoil
The evidence and proof
Of these restraints
Always leaning steady
As far as I can see
Never falling out
Always with sure stability
Paint it on a wall
As big as a square
Your ability to break
From these constraints
To keep it in moderation
Always thinking
Being barely adequate
Or just plain ordinary.

Zero

BE AT ZERO
NEITHER HERE NOR THERE
NOT TOO MUCH
JUST ENOUGH TO KEEP STANDING STRAIGHT
SO MUCH CONFUSION
ALWAYS HARD TO BREATH
YOU SAY TAKE IT EASY
MAKE IT SEEM RIGHT
BUT IN THE END
IT WILL NOT MATTER
BECAUSE WE WILL BOTH BE DEAD
STAND ON YOUR BALANCE
TRY NOT TO SWAY
YOUR FALL WILL BE LIKE ROLLING THUNDER
CRASHING, LIKE A STONE AGAINST WATER
STAY IN THE MIDDLE
KEEP FROM DEVIATING TO EITHER SIDE
I SAY SWEAT IT OUT
UNTIL YOU STAND ON NOTHING
BECAUSE IN THE END
WE ALL WANT TO LIVE
IT'S WHAT SEEMS RIGHT.

Hurry Up And Wait

My mind is always racing, like it's going a thousand miles per hour. I'm constantly looking for a short cut, an efficient and productive way of accomplishing things. This state of mind can be very hazardous to your health or it can be brilliant, depending on when you use it. I used to have a job that required being in the proper frame of mind or you wouldn't go home alive. It also required precision and accuracy to properly complete the tasks. The pressures of time and money are always factors that affect your performance, especially when you're all by yourself.

It seems that you never enjoy anything when you are moving this fast. In my case, I don't remember anything. My impatience and my will to get through what I have to do, does not allow me to enjoy the experience. A lot of bad things can happen very quickly when you're in this mode and making irrational decisions does not help in any way either. There is a time to be expedient and efficient. I learned very quickly in the Marines that reacting out of instinct is more beneficial for everyone. Nonetheless, this is another quality that has been transferred from the military world to the civilian world.

New Moon

It's long overdue
Time to move
In your direction
Without uncertainty or indecision

Always something
Getting in the way
Not you but me
Keeping myself from advancing

Like the birth of a new life
The awakening of a dormant motion
The appearance of a brilliant new moon

Always looking
For something new
Not stale or faded
But pure and untainted

Unchanging and everlasting
Remaining to the very end

May it cast over you
As you reach ultimate capacity
To get up and move.

PIECES

Pick you up
Shattered and broken
All over the ground
Never again to be spoken

Wishing you've never fallen
Back in time
To save you
Bring it back again

Into tiny pieces
I found you
Standing around
Waiting for the moment
To become what you wished for

Try to put you back
Thinking of ways
To bring it together
Never once to even consider

Fragments of this
To help you
Come back, come back
That's the way it is.

ADD IT UP

A Lump of dirt
Waiting for someone
To use or kick
A pile of trash
Ready for the burning
To light on fire
I've given up
Trying to add it up
Take nothing
And turn it into something
Nothing into something
Over and over I play it
Figure out
Why I'm wasted
Let the rains fall
And watch this mound
Slowly fade away
Throw this junk far away
Through the tiny
Tiny front
Saw you change colors
Right before my eyes
Not knowing
What the score is.

STUCK

Here I am
Stuck
Between here and now
Let me squeeze
Everything inside
So I can get by
Signals and flashes
Everyone taking their turn
In all directions
As I watch and burn
A thousand miles an hour
But barely moving
Need to get where I'm going
Might not get there
Try not to side blind
Won't be able to explain
Because I don't want to
And have no alibi
Minutes pass the hour
Seems I've been here forever
Shadows crossing over
My head and shoulder
See nothing but red
I know it's the way
The direction I have to take
Straight, straight ahead
So many of you
Where do you come from?
Where are you going?
.... Am I like you?

HASTE

The day
Of my moment with you
I went back
Remembered
How I needed more time

Took your clock
From the green wall
Hung it on my chest
So it wouldn't fall

Sheets spread
From here to there
To cover me
From my toes
All the way to my hair

To make haste
So much time to waste
Every minute of the hour
To satisfy a craving taste

Everything I desired
So dedicated
Bringing it all together
As anticipated.

Just can't stand it!

Running and running
A thousand miles an hour
When I stop
I'll be spinning and spinning
A thousand miles more

Keep moving
This way and that way
Always losing
Each and every other way

Just can't stand it
I really want to stop it
Just can't stand it
I really want to end it

Out of control
Losing my direction
Never find a place
To help my situation

Working and working
Never get my fill
If I stop
In two I'll be broken

Caught between the lines
Jumping and diving
Avoiding every stone
Falling from the skies

Roaming and raging
In a space that confines
Losing my energy
And a sweat to burn my eyes.

Reflection

I do a lot of daydreaming. I think about all the wrong turns I took and I tell myself how I can make it better. At times I have a melancholic episode and other times I feel guilt. It's mostly when I'm driving a long distance, or when I go for a jog. People say it's a good idea to do some sort of inventory before you go to bed - it keeps you on your toes and it keeps you closer to the ground. I like to give myself " at-a-boys" once in awhile; a mental lists of the good things I accomplished throughout the day. Sometimes I have a hard time getting to sleep.

A wise man once told me to be kind to people because you never know what kind of battles they are facing. He also told me that it wasn't a good idea to sleep alone, that a man shouldn't be all by himself because he gets into trouble that way. The most memorable thing he ever told me was to share whatever fortune I may acquire with those that are less fortunate. I really think that overcoming trials and hardships builds character. It makes you wiser. You put into practice all the knowledge that comes from frustrations and accomplishments. I like to daydream!

You Are

Down to my last resort
Wrapped a knot
Tied it around my chest

In my final breath
I gasped her name
With nothing underneath

End of a picture
Stamped forever in my mind
I will never remember

But you are
You are everything
I desire

Runaway with you
Climb inside
Never come out
Fall away and get lost
Never to be found

Live forever
To see the life
And fulfill the promise

It's understood
Actions are louder
Completely satisfied

I'll take you
Wrap you up
Never let you go.

Your Own

Have it your way
Take this opportunity
Because I'm forbidding you to stay

Take my hand
And always agree
To follow through with your pain

Never a single minute
Without a doubt
Never hesitate to take that step

Make it your own
All by yourself
Just like you started

Nothing gained
Nothing learned

I'll see you again
Front and center
Under the shadow
Of what was meant to be

Make it count
We've got until tomorrow
To give it your all

Because we don't know
We just don't know.

Secrets

I'm on my way
On a road
No one's ever
Taken before

Bury my chin
Deep in my chest
Fix my frown
Hope the sky doesn't come down

Expectations
As I walk
Through the treachery
Anticipations
Of being marked
In every way

You will see
Heavenly transformations
As the beautiful
Journey ends

Your subconscious
Explanations
The dispersions
Of your mortal confessions

The secrets
Will no longer
Protect you
Give up what you have
So you may see the truth.

Slowly Pay Time

Slowly pay time
Not enough to spend
I want to take it because
I can't really fake it

Palms together
Walking towards us
Looking up
Hoping to be with us

To listen
Take and remember
This little moment

For eternity and forever

Your words
Traveling on the wind
Jumping off
Pushing me to an end

To give you
My empty Pocket
All or nothing
Is all you're going to get

The pictures
Capturing everything
To remind us
The truth…. And just us.

LAST MISTAKE

This will be my last mistake
If it's the only thing I do
Who can bear such heartache?
One after another
This chain I have to break
Is there anything real anymore?
I want to ride the wind
May it take me where no one goes
To reach the heights of heaven
Visit a place where honey flows
I want to get high
To reach a place no one knows
This will be the last mistake
Even if I have to crawl into a hole
Must hide from the heartache
Never deal with another
These bonds I must break
And search for something pure.

You Had It Coming

They shut you down
Restrained with iron and stone
Striped your skin
Didn't know the trouble you were in
Disguised with the world
Miles and miles you've traveled
Now you're naked
And we see who you really are
You had it coming
Now you get what you deserve
Crying your tears
Pounding your fists
You had it coming
Deserve a whole lot more
Take it in the chest
Because you had it coming
I see your struggle
Below the surface with no air
Open your eyes
And see that I'm under
Why are you still alive?
Tell me how you did it
Who released from your cell
Who broke your spell?
I look up
I open my eyes
I see your freedom
Above the surface
As I fight with myself
Down here
Face to face

BEST YEARS

Came to the realization
That my time is at hand
And I've discovered
The best years are gone

Never had a guide
Never received proper instruction
Just went
On a big rollercoaster ride

Could've been anything
That's what they would say
Listen to my reason
And you'll be on your way

The conclusion of this story
Begins with an end
You'll never have these years
Ever again

I've seen the pictures
The memories attached
All alone I stand
With the best years gone

How It Really Is

Reality is sometimes deceiving. The way things really are is something I've had a hard time with. I remember coming home from serving six years in the Marines; I could not believe the things I came home to. A part of you tries to understand but the other half wants to fix it very quickly. You're constantly fighting with yourself about everything, talking to yourself like a maniac and then running straight into a wall. Then you come to a realization: that's just the way it is. You can't really do anything about it; you have to let the boat sink sometimes. That in itself is so contradictory.... and I find myself going through the cycle again.

Expectations can really kill you. Assumptions can make you look like an ass. And ignorance is soul numbing. The truth is, nobody wants to hear it. Nobody wants to hear how it really is; nobody desires to seek the real issue of things. My truth has been a matter of life and death. A while back, I chose to listen to someone tell me what was wrong with me. I had the pleasure of listening to what they called "shortcomings" or in other words, character defects. From that point I knew the truth about myself and how it really is.

WALKING ON HEADSTONES

I look to the sky
See where I want to be
I look to the ground
And see where I will be
Took a look again
Nothing more to complain

I was walking
Walking all over you
I was walking
Right above you

So many times
I have fallen So many times
I wanted to stay there

Broken bones
Fractured dreams
Empty promises
That I can't see

Yard of posterity
Acres of the unknown
To whom do they cry
When it's not seen

So many times
I have chosen
So many times
I wanted to lie there

I was walking
Walking all over you
I was walking
Right above you

INCURABLE

Heard about my fate
Could not believe
That I would not be able
To continue with this

Walked along the street
Saw gods and idols
Standing all in line
Awaiting my decision

Chose the one
Humble and simple
Colorless and kind

She took my hands
Raised them to the sky
Patched the hole on my side

Closing her eyes
Took me on a walk
Towards the love I once had

Took me in
Started where we left off
Forgiven and accepted
Once again my spirit lifted

Offered many thanks
Kept on receiving
From the abundance of my giving

Treated my affliction
The mighty doctor with care
Removed my addiction

Heard about my fate
Could not believe
That I would not be able
To continue with this....

KEEPING TRACK

Have you ever been there?
Hitting the mark
Right in the middle
Hoping you'll stop

Aiming in your direction
Looking through a wire
Calculate your step
Standing up straight

Counting your rocks
Keeping track
Of where you're going
Not knowing where it ends

In the center
Right on target
Between me and you
Tearing it all apart

Paste it black
No one knows
What you're looking at

You've become greater
Watching the distance
From far away
Into something better.

SEE NOW

Can I capture my thoughts for you?
I want you to see what I see
Every spoken injustice
And every moment of spiritual violence
To see the kind of expression
That breaks my heart
And every bit of maltreated innocence
Impatient and intolerant
Putting off your opportunity
To make space
In your eternal resting place
Take a good look
You've taken more
Than what you've given
A little heavier on your side
With all that good living
Don't look away now
Running....
Will never shatter that mirror
See what I see....
See what I see now
It's right here

The proof we've been waiting for
Recorded in your memory
For all to see when you show yourself
Using anything and everyone
To ease your landing
From the torture of stepping
And grinding
Who can possibly help?
Selfish little bastard
Who do you think you are?
To make you realize
What we think about you
We have to cut you down
Replant and make you new again
Now you know
Your numbers been called
And all that's left
Take your piece
And hope it's not in contempt.

Changes

Never wanted this
To sit alone and wonder
Why it all changes
So hard
So hard to move
Take my heavy heart
Bring a new start
Don't le it fall apart
It's so hard
So hard to lose
Brought it all together
To see it go
And I don't know
It's just so hard
So hard to leave
Fallen to pieces I've given up
And all I know
It's so hard
So damn hard to take
Never thought it would be like this
I wish you were in my place
These changes
Taking up so much space.

ROTATION

I'm tired of paying for you
After so much time
It all comes back
To keep me under
Such obligation

Why wasn't it me?
Why have you chosen?
That day
It should've been me
To die that day

Nine times over
Recorded in my brain
The moments that I will never
Be able to contain

The cost of my mistakes
Cannot be paid
By my own hands
But restitution
With innocent recompense

One of these days
There will be no return
No way to restore
Or any kind of reparation

The damage will be too great
And your losses
Will be worth more
Than your original state

Let me be
Keep it going
Because I have a funny feeling
I'm about to intervene.

Re: Back Again

It's very strange how I find myself in the same situations time after time. I think it happens because I haven't learned my lesson yet, so it must present itself again until I get a passing grade. I've always thought I was a fast learner at many things. I'm good at learning mechanical stuff; I do very well working with my hands but everything else, forget about it. I would like to think that I'm great at relationships, but I really have a hard time with the social side of my life. I've never really learned how to maintain and nurture any type of relationships.

Sometimes I voluntarily want to go back. I miss the camaraderie, the adventure, adrenaline and the sense of belonging. When these thoughts come around, it's usually because there is nothing exciting happening and I crave those moments. To not have a sense of purpose can be debilitating, especially if there is no support system. Wanting to be right back in it also means that there is something unsettled within. For some reason, I think I can do what I used to do. I'm holding on to that glorious momentary time of youth. But I don't desire to go back to all that pain that goes with it.

RELATIVITY

I want to see how it ends
Will it be fair?
Are you capable of making amends?
I know I can turn it on and off
Flip the switch
And I'm right back in it
I've chosen and I've decided
It's not you
But what comes first

Differences to you they are
Just a matter of time
Before you understand
Change only if you want to
Or if it's worth your while
Be a better person
An example

Someone to look up to
I don't understand because I'm not wise
Can't control because I'm not strong
All I know is how to get it done
Going a short distance
And following through
Some get by with a strand of hair
Others live a boring
And meaningless constant
You don't have what it takes
Not just for me
But for everyone else

It always plays out
Me, you and for them
Tragedy to give your body
Not of your mind
In and out at your convenience
You say take it slow
But cover yourself with my soul.

REMNANT

A single underline
A word from you
A final act
Will be mine

The thread
That holds my world
With yours
Is about to snap

Only thing left
Is the evidence
This proof
A remnant of my future with you

A common title
The name of my place
Is the same here
.... And there

This single thread
That's holding my world with yours
Is about to break....
About to snap in two

A constant reminder
To keep you on course
Is the same here
.... And everywhere.

Rebirth

Afraid of what's not happening
Confused in my own misery
Many things spoken

Standing in the same place
Trying to figure out
Why I picture your face

A fresh start.... No way
Same old tears
Going through the changes
Revisiting my old fears

Can't see much
Wish I were numb
Going through the motions
Empty feelings and such

I can pace your birth
Day in day out
Wanting you near
See what its really worth

Impossible to go back
Lay it all up
Take your chance
And pick up the slack.

RED FLAG

I THREW MY HANDS IN THE AIR
TRYING TO FIGURE OUT
WHAT I DID THIS TIME
CAN'T DO THIS OR THAT
DON'T SPEAK
YOU'RE WAY OUT OF LINE
DO WHAT IS PROPER
SO THEY CAN KEEP TAKING
EVERYTHING YOU'VE WORKED FOR
MY EVIDENCE
THE NUMBERS WRITTEN DOWN
ALL THE BRUISES
TO YOU WILL BE UNKNOWN
BUT I WILL THROW
MY HANDS UP IN THE AIR AGAIN
SO YOU CAN SEE
THE RED FLAG
MY WARNING TO YOU
LET ME BE
AND LET ME SPEAK
WHAT MORE CAN YOU TAKE
EVERYTHING IN MY HANDS
AND MY RIGHT TO BREATHE
I DARE YOU TO APPROACH
AND INVADE
LIKE MANY TIMES BEFORE
TO TAKE EVERYTHING
WE'VE WORKED FOR
YOU GIVE ME NO CHOICE
BUT TO WARN YOU
OVER AND OVER
LET ME BE
OVER AND OVER
LET ME SPEAK
SO YOU CAN SEE.

RELIC

Strangers come to your door
Refuge and comfort
Is what they say
They are looking for

Open up and let them in
Invite them to your banquet
Make sure
They never need again

Protect the innocent
Take care of what is sacred
The relic entrusted
To never be taken

There will be
Those that will see
Make sure
It will be taken away

Lift your head
Take your stone
Toss it
Hit them
Right in the eye

Open up and let them in
See if they like
What you've done
They'll never come in again

Residue

Once again
I've tried to put my finger on it
Try to find my place
Gave you what you needed
Never asked anything in return

You're all the same
Think you can
But you can't
Can't even cross the street

Where do I go?
Not looking for answers
Just for a fair fight

In every corner
I hope for the best
But I find the residue
Evidence of what had to be
Your ultimate test

You've gone too far
Think you can
But you can't
Can't even be discrete

Where are we?
Here's my answer
Keep your eyes open
It will be all night.

My Jane

I have noticed that I have written more poems about my encounters with my significant other than any other kinds of poems. They are not all sad, depressing or angry. Some of them are quite romantic, I think. A woman can motivate you to do a lot of crazy things. I heard someone say that behind every successful man, there is a reason for his success, his significant other. I think that is true. I also think the opposite. Either way, women have a way to stimulate men to the point of insanity, good and bad. Think of all the songs and novels that have been written about love and hate between men and women.

The old cliché, "you can't live with them, you can't live without them", is certainly true. My grandfather was married to my grandmother almost sixty years and they couldn't stand each other at times, but they also couldn't be apart for long. He stole her from her house when he wasn't allowed to be around her. He married her and provided for her with a lot of sacrifice and hard work. Men will do the craziest things for love. For me, written words will do for now. I don't plan on stealing anything.

Romadore

In so many ways
We are perfect
For each other
Her soft kisses
Speak
Of our future together
Tell her I love her
How do I tell her?
I can't live without her
What can I say?
What can I do?
Tell her
Tell her that I need her
A moment of romance and adoration

In the space between her heart and mine
When she looks at me, smiles of grace and
Gratitude.... She comforts me when she holds
Me by the hand.

You Know

YOU KNOW
EVERYBODY KNOWS
YOU'VE HAD ALL YOU CAN HAVE

FROM A SETTING SUN
TO THE SHINIEST STAR
AND EVERYTHING IN BETWEEN

THE SOFTEST TOUCH
TO THE KINDEST SMILE
TO HAVE LOVED MUCH

BUT IT DOESN'T MATTER
NOTHING REALLY HELPS
ONLY YOU CAN CHANGE
WHAT WILL HAPPEN NEXT

BOUNCING OFF THE GROUND
I FOUND MYSELF
LOOKING FORWARD

DON'T REALLY KNOW
WHY THIS HAPPENS
YOU TAKE WHAT YOU WANT
AND NEVER REALLY EXPLAIN

I WONDER WHERE
YOU LAY TONIGHT
ARE YOU COLD?
OR DO YOU WEAR A WARM COAT?

PROOF

You finally went away
Closed your lips
Opened the ears
And had nothing to say

Something mean and ugly
Between you and I
Terribly shared
Never give it another try

The eyes never lie
Stare into them deeply
But what you did
Spoke to me.... Immensely

Take a moment to consider
Everything you had
At your beckon call
You will always remember

To prove to who
Doesn't matter
Just wait and see
Give it all up
Because....
You don't have anything to give me.

GRAY

Why is it never enough?
Always want it my way
Never satisfied

Give me a smile
Shake my hand
I want it all

Where do I stop?
When shall I continue?
Don't know what's right

Like the color gray
Neither Black nor white
Treading in the middle
That's where I want to stay

Meet me there
You and me Gray
Lost in between
That's where I want to stay

I'll wait
Just don't know how long
Before someone else
Comes along

More and more
You give
More and more
I'll take.

Little Things

If I could read your mind
I would know your intentions
I could keep you from wandering
As if you were blind

And where do we start?
What can I possibly say?
To help you get through
Without falling apart

It makes a lot of sense
The advice I give my friends
Don't let them overcome you
These little things

Trouble them....
So they won't overthrow you

One way or another
The time will come
When you have to stand
And start over

No matter what
Cheer up, it won't take long
Lift yourself up
You're not the only one

It makes no sense
These little things
Consuming my life
In my time of innocence.

Don't Mind Waiting

I saw a picture yesterday
Running across the finish line
What seemed so real
Almost broke my will

With a shiny burden on my chest
And a prize on my head
Proved to be
Better than the rest

It hurt so bad
My imagination tossing
Taking it, caressing it
And feeling it in my hand

But I don't mind waiting
It can take forever
I've already won
Because we're always together

Keep hanging on
Take this little ounce
And tie it
To yourself

All I need
Is that picture from yesterday
To keep running your way
But I don't mind waiting.

TROUBLE

Took a step outside
Had to look for myself
Wanted to see
What was coming down the street

Nothing but trouble
You're going to give me trouble

Lord almighty
Couldn't believe
What was staring
Straight in my eye

The best kind
Of trouble to be in

Like a storm
Raging in the darkness
Unafraid of danger
Contemplating complications

Nothing but trouble
You're going to give me trouble

Dreamy kisses
A sensual touch
Can't really handle
Your motions and such

The best kind
Of trouble to be in

Took a step outside
Had to look for myself
Wanted to see
You coming back to me.

About the Book

These poems were written out of necessity. I came to a point in my life where I asked myself who I really was, but I didn't have an answer. I had very hard questions about my courage, integrity, self worth, and especially my direction in life. I have accumulated so many experiences in my short life that sometimes I feel like an old man. The truth is, these experiences had molded me into someone with knowledge and just a hint of wisdom. So I wrote everything down, every emotion I felt coupled with every memory and every thought that provoked words from my mouth. The hardest thing to do is express the truth, especially if it is not pleasant.

Jorge Aguayo is a combat-decorated Marine who served with the Third Marine Division as an infantryman. He participated in Desert Storm, Desert Shield from 1990-1991 assisting with the liberation of Kuwait. *Vita* is Aguayo's first book.